ELLEN K. KUZWAYO was born o
Nchu, east of Bloemfontein. Af
she attended Adams College a
Natal, where she remained for five years, obtaining a teacher's diploma. She returned home and taught at Thaba-
Nchu, then at Heilbron, also in the Free State, Rusten-
burg in the old Transvaal, and finally in Johannesburg.
When the Nationalist government introduced Bantu Education in 1954, she left teaching and trained as a social
worker instead, a profession she still informally practises
to this day.

She has worked extensively with youth clubs and women's
groups. The Zamane Soweto Sisters' Centre, which she
helped to establish in the eighties, still instructs women and
girls in various skills and crafts.

This is her third book. The first, *Call Me Woman*, an auto-
biography, was published in 1984 and was translated into
seven European languages. The second, *Sit Down and
Listen*, a collection of short stories, appeared in two foreign
editions.

In 1994 Dr Ellen Kuzwayo was elected to the first demo-
cratic parliament of South Africa, as an ANC MP. Her home
is in Orlando West, Soweto. She is grandmother to six
grandchildren.

AFRICAN WISDOM

ELLEN K. KUZWAYO
*A personal collection
of Setswana proverbs*

Kwela Books

Lino cut on cover and figures inside by Patrick Holo
Cover design by Jürgen Fomm
Typography by Nazli Jacobs
Set in New Century Schoolbook
Printed and bound by National Book Printers
Drukkery Street, Goodwood, Western Cape
First edition, first printing 1998

ISBN 0-7957-0083-0

SINCERE THANKS TO:

Betty Wolpert – who kept reminding me of my intention to write about the impact of proverbs in the black community in South Africa;

Professor Es'kia Mphahlele – who shared with me some of his expertise when we reviewed the original manuscript;

Blanche Ramaphakela – who helped to locate words in the dictionary, to decipher words not clearly written, and for the general support she gave with joy;

Joyce Seroke – who responded immediately to a request when I called on her;

Peteni and Boitumelo Kuzwayo – my two youngest grand-children, who were always considerate when I stopped them from visiting me when I needed time to write;

the Maggie Magaba Trust, staff and trustees – who accommo-dated me when I was under pressure, working on this book;

my children Justice Moloto, Godfrey and Eunice Kuzwayo – for their unexpressed yet very obvious support through my writing career;

Clive and Irene Menell – who provided me with much needed transport and for their support and encourage-ment of my literary endeavours;

and Bheki Mathabathe – for typing this manuscript as a gift.

I dedicate this third book to
my mother Mmutsi Emma Tsimatsima,
born Makgothi, first married to Merafe.

She constantly used proverbs as a form of guidance,
reprimand, and teaching in our upbringing.
Without this foundation I could never have emerged
the person I am today.

Thank you.
I shall cherish those memories of early childhood.

To mother
with Much Love

Proverbs: an additional educational system

Looking back on my life, it suddenly dawned on me that, possibly from my birth, and certainly from the age of five years, I was exposed to two distinct systems of education. While I consciously embraced one of these systems, I was hardly aware of the other.

From the age of six or seven, I attended school at Thabapatchoa Primary in the district of Thaba-Nchu in the Free State. This school was on the farm of my maternal grandfather, Jeremiah Gopolang Makgothi. At the turn of the century, he himself had built the school with the assistance of his immediate family and the community of other families living on the farm.

This was the only farm in the area which provided a school for Africans. The few coloured children living on his farm and on the surrounding white-owned farms also attended Thabapatchoa Primary.

In passing, the farm was left to the other grandchildren and me. In 1974, the National Party under the leadership of John Vorster declared it a "Black Spot" and dispossessed us of the farm. We are in the process of claiming it back.

The school was run and administered by one teacher. In those years, beginners attending school were provided with small reading books known as *Sepelete sa Setswana*, which meant Setswana spelling books for Setswana-speaking pupils. Indeed, inside of a year those young pupils became proficient in reading, writing and spelling.

These Setswana spelling books were very simple, dull and without pictures, printed in black ink on ordinary white paper. There was nothing exciting about them, yet they provided us with welcome (though monotonous) reading material. The less quick pupils recited these books in a parrot-like manner, without catching the meaning of what they read.

We used to read everything as if it was a recitation, without grasping the meaning.

The same process was followed in the teaching of Arithmetic. We learnt to recite multiplication tables up to 12 x in a monotonous sing-song manner. We sang like parrots:

Two times one is two
two times two is four
two times three is six
two times four is eight ...

or:

Three times one is three
three times two is six
three times three is nine
three times four is twelve ...

Another important subject, though, in those years was Scripture. Here we were subjected to memorising chunks of Biblical writing. The most popular was Psalm 23 – an assignment we memorised in Setswana or English, depending on the standard you were in. So one year we would recite:

Jehova ke modisa wa me
Ga nkitla ke tlhoka sepe ...

and the next:

The Lord is my shepherd
I shall not want ...

The best loved of all school activities, however, was singing and music. Many of the songs we sang were incomprehensible. We did not understand a word, but enjoyed the accompanying actions and hand movements all the same. I still remember one little song about Japan:

Good evening, my dear little maidens
We are the gay little girls from Japan
We come from a beautiful country ...

We loved this song, because we wore special costumes, which included fans for fanning ourselves. Looking back, I realise that our teachers could have used these songs to teach us Geography or History. But we simply sang them for enjoyment. Together with our teacher we also composed our own songs, like this one:

Thichere ena ke ya rona
– This is our teacher

E tswa kwa sekolong sa Thaba-Nchu
– He comes from Thaba-Nchu school

E tlile go ruta, e tlile go ruta
– He has come to teach, he has come to teach

E tlile go ruta lefoko la Modimo
– He has come to teach the word of God

In addition to formal learning, our schooling also provided us with the opportunity to make friends, to play, to socialise and to develop in all directions. The long hours at school compelled us to bring something to eat at break. Pupils from the village of farm workers generally brought lovely sour porridge, known as "motogo-wa-seqhaqhabola", in silvery containers with handles. These containers were clean and shining. We, on the other hand, brought butter-and-jam sandwiches to school. Soon, we were exchanging our lunch of sandwiches for motogo-wa-seqhaqhabola, which we greatly enjoyed, whilst our friends loved the sandwiches. That dish of seqhaqhabola is a favourite Sesotho dish. To this day, I'll give anything to eat it. It is delicious.

These memories of my formal schooling still give me great joy. To this day, I value and treasure it as part of the foundation of who I am today.

It was thus with great sadness that I watched as "Bantu Education" was introduced. The legacy of Bantu Education saw many students leaving school and drifting into the streets or becoming unemployable. In the seventies, as most people know, Bantu Education led to an eruption of violence as school children rebelled against an inferior and oppressive education system.

As a consequence, violence and lawlessness increased dramatically in the past two decades. Although I am fully convinced that the blame for today's violence and crime should rest squarely on the shoulders of the old Nationalist government, the violence in my community has given me many sleepless nights. As I turned these problems over and over in my mind, my thoughts suddenly drifted back to the time when I was young. And this was when a second, less formalised system of education came back to me.

Proverbs: our culture, our heritage

I recall my mother's voice which called me to order, and often ended with some strong proverb to express the gravity of the wrong done. In those years, parents' reprimands were taken seriously and with respect. It was common practice for my mother to send me off soul-searching with a proverb. That proverb said it all.

As I write this now, I can hear her voice: "Tsholofelo" – her favourite name for me, meaning "hope" – "ngwana yo o sa reetseng molao wa bagolo, o tla thanya lomapo lo le tsebeng."

This is one of the commonest proverbs used by adults when they reprimand youth. The literal meaning is that a child who does not heed the elders' warning and advice will suffer the rapture of his or her eardrum: Children who are disobedient will meet tragedy.

Of the many interactions I had with my mother, those many years ago, one stands out with clarity. I remember the occasion when Mother sent me to the main road, about twenty yards away from the homestead, to invite a passing group of seasonal work-seekers home for a meal. She instructed me to take a container along and collect dry cow-dung for making a fire. I was then to prepare the meal for the group of work-seekers.

The thought of making an open fire outside at midday, cooking in a large three-legged pot in that intense heat, was sufficient to upset even an angel. I did not manage to conceal my feelings from my mother, and after serving the group, she called me to the veranda, where she usually sat to attend to her sewing and knitting.

Looking straight into my eyes, she said, "Tsholofelo, why did you sulk when I requested you to prepare a meal for those poor destitute people?"

Despite my attempt to deny her allegation, and using the heat of the fire and the sun as an excuse for my alleged behaviour, Mother, giving me a firm look, said, "Lonao ga lo na nko"– "A foot has no nose." It means: You cannot detect what trouble may lie ahead for you. Had I denied this group of people a meal, it may have happened that in my travels some time in the future, I found myself at the mercy of some of those very individuals.

As if that was not enough to shame me, Mother continued, "Motho ke motho ka motho yo mongwe". The literal meaning: A person is a person because of another person. Its closest English equivalent is probably: "No man is an island."

This particular proverb is found among all ethnic groups in South Africa. I believe it is similar to the concept of "Ubuntu" in the Nguni languages, isiZulu and isiXhosa, and "Botho" in the Sotho languages, Setswana, Sesotho and Sepedi.

This one proverb lays down the principles and values of "human" interaction for all African inhabitants of southern Africa. I would not be surprised if it is also found in the rest of the continent.

In African culture, "Botho" expresses the interdependence of all people regardless of age, sex or social standing. When we in South Africa discuss the violence of the present day, we often end up saying: "What has become of Botho?"

I am haunted by the prevailing violence; the abuse of young girls, the rape of young and old women, the car-theft, the senseless killings of people … I sometimes wake up in the middle of the night and ask myself: "What has happened to Botho? How can it be restored?"

As I grappled with the frightening violence and racked my mind for remedies, I had to conclude that any effective remedy would have to combine a variety of solutions. And the language of proverbs struck me as one of the instruments, which could help.

A note on "vulgar" proverbs

Proverbs can be classified into three major categories according to their functional duties. There are proverbs which are used to express statement of fact; others are used to express caution and to reprimand, and the rest are loaded with messages of guidance.

In all these categories, it is possible to find proverbs that use seemingly uncouth language or "vulgar" images. To people foreign to African culture these proverbs may seem obscene, and thus unacceptable, whilst inside the community where they originated, they may carry a totally different message: a message loaded with warning against some danger; a message of alert against abusing or undermining other people.

The apparently crude language or image used to bring home the meaning of these proverbs is always acceptable to people inside that community. This is because these proverbs convey a valid message within the social and cultural context of the particular community.

In this category, for example, are proverbs which convey their meaning by mentioning the male or female organs. In others the image of faeces is used to get across the seriousness of the situation. In the community where such proverbs are used, it is the message conveyed and not the seemingly vulgar terms used to do so, which is important. The circumstances under which a term is used determine whether it is offensive or not. Thus obscene language used when individuals or groups quarrel is considered offensive, while the same terms used in idiomatic expression are not.

When I was young, strong and seemingly crude reprimand was not seen as vulgar by those reprimanded. More often than not, it was taken to heart, and seriously pondered over. As a girl, for example, I was expected to take part in the household chores – to make early-morning tea or coffee for my parents, to sweep the lapa, and to fetch water from the community well. Above all, I was expected to wake up before sunrise to complete these chores before I went to school. All girls of that era had to do this. Failure led to wrath and anger from adults. Misbehaviour earned me a very harsh proverb from my mother. I still remember her saying: "Fa o sa reetsa kgakollo tsa me, o tla ja masepa a thaka tsa gago" – "If you don't heed my advice, you will eat your peer-group's faeces."

This proverb was widely used in rural areas then, and is probably still commonly used by parents if children disregard their guidance. However, today, I cannot use these proverbs in reprimanding my urbanised grandchildren or others of their age-group, lest I am accused of abusing them. What a shame and what a pity.

Proverbs: our traditional teachings

As I have mentioned, in my upbringing, and in the upbringing of my contemporaries, we were fed, guided, reprimanded and moulded by our parents and elders through the language of proverbs. We received our formal education at school, but we also received another education – through our constant exposure to proverbs. In the early era of stable indigenous communities in the southern African region, proverbs had great influence over the social and cultural tapestry of community institutions. Family life, social services, politics, economic activity and religion were greatly influenced by proverbs, as were all community activities, be they joyful celebrations or solemn commemorations.

We need to give the youth of our country a fresh taste of those cultural values which can inspire and guide them. Proverbs are our heritage – to be preserved, promoted and treasured. The time has come to review and re-evaluate traditional African values, cultural practices, and idiomatic and proverbial language. Different indigenous communities have proverbs peculiar to their own geographic setting; to uphold their values, morals, and their overall way of life. All these lay down guidelines and expectations for the whole community, regardless of age, sex or standing in the community. These proverbs express deep-seated feelings, emotions, values and duties, all of which go to determine a social moral code and ethical values which lay down a common foundation for human interaction and relationship throughout a particular community. Some of these proverbs set social standards for the entire black population of southern Africa. These traditional teachings should be included in the curriculum of schools in our country.

At the point where I came to this conclusion, I started to put on paper as many proverbs as I could remember. As my list grew longer, I realised I was a moving encyclopaedia of Setswana proverbs, and that the list should be preserved for future generations. Discouraging thoughts intruded. For instance, 80 per cent of the African community cannot read; those youths who can read will probably reject and despise a book on proverbs; educated Africans may see the book as backward ...

Finally, I dismissed all those thoughts and decided to write this book and hand it over to fate.

I have no doubt that proverbs will go a long way towards addressing the devastating violence and crime caused by a lack of values and cultural pride. There are many proverbs which are not in this book. But the few included here amply illustrate their importance. Proverbs contribute to character-building and self-respect. They contribute to the spiritual well-being of a community.

This book is written in the spirit of helping my community wake up from the oppression and depression we have suffered; for us to realise we have a heritage which compares favourably with that of other race groups. Our common heritage is based on "Botho", based on "Ubuntu" – a spirit which lays a foundation for the recognition, respect, and the reaffirmation of each other's humanity.

THE PROVERBS

Each of the seventy odd proverbs appears in Setswana first; then a literal English translation is given, followed by the interpretation. Where possible an English equivalent is given, because sometimes the very same wisdom is also contained in an English idiom or expression – which goes to show that there are some universal truths found in cultures and languages all over the world. Only the way in which a particular culture and language express them is unique.

To facilitate consulting this book, the proverbs have been loosely arranged according to theme, rather than the type of proverb. It is not at all a strict or academic categorisation, and the same proverb can just as easily be listed under more than one heading. A fair amount of overlapping occurs and proverbs are by their nature often ambiguous.

The important thing to keep in mind is that proverbs expressing a statement of fact may be found under the same heading as others which caution or reprimand, and others still which contain messages of guidance.

TO START OFF, let's have a look at some of the proverbs in which food and water feature, and what they tell us. Normally, eating is a social activity, and in a rural environment where people are almost totally dependent on nature for their food, eating and having enough to eat is of central concern. Various proverbs are inspired by the necessity to eat or to make provision:

Tsie e fofa ka moswang

A locust keeps flying with a full stomach

You can keep going if you have have eaten;
in other words, if you have made proper provision

Sedibana pele ga se ikanngwe

The fountain ahead cannot be trusted

*Do not trust that you will find a fountain somewhere
along your journey, make provision in life*

Go ja ga go die, go dia go dira

It is work, not eating, which delays

*Eating takes less time than working, make sure you eat so
that you will be able to carry on working – said of someone
who keeps on working and does not stop to eat*

EATING HEALTHY FOOD is clearly necessary, so having to eat unwholesome stuff is used in two proverbs that warn against disobedience and acting irresponsibly. Herewith a very important theme is introduced, that of the family:

O tla ja masepa a thaka tsa gago
You will eat your peer-group's shit
You will end up looking towards your equals for advice, having refused to heed your parents' guidance as a child. As a reward you will have to accept whatever they give you

Sebodu se jewa ke beng
The rotten thing is eaten by its owners
It is the immediate family that suffers the repercussions of the evil or wrong deeds of a family member

The family

In all close-knit societies, especially in the African communities in southern Africa, the extended family and the relationship between parents and children are of paramount importance. It is therefore not surprising that many proverbs expressing a statement of fact reflect on this:

Legala le tsala molora
Coal gives birth to ash
A successful and gifted family or parent may produce a misfit or an unsuccessful off-spring

Mmangwana o tshwara thipa ka fa bogaleng
A child's mother catches the knife at the sharp end
A mother will risk any danger to save or protect her off-spring

Ke mpampetsa sa mpa sa mokotla ke a se bolaya
I pamper the one from the belly, from the back I destroy
You care for those you were born with, those from your immediate family, but towards those you meet later in life, you feel no loyalty

Ga bo boi ga go lliwe
At the coward's home, there is no weeping
A family who is cautious and fearful is saved pain and weeping

Molato o sekwa ke ditshoswane
A case is argued by ants
Evil done to parents can be settled by their off-spring

Mmatla kgwana o e lebisa gaabo
The heifer-seeker destines it for home
Make sure that the good results of your efforts end up at home;
"Charity begins at home"

Kgomo go gatana tsa saka le le lengwe
Only cattle from the same kraal step on each other
You tend to hurt those closest to you

BUT FAMILY RELATIONSHIPS can get complicated, two of the proverbs I recall warn:

Mma-poo ga a nyalwe
Mrs Bull never gets married
Be warned about getting married to the mother of a male child – the male child may grow up rebellious and may reject his stepfather

Mona morula o mona o le mongwe
The one who sucks a marula fruit sucks only from that one tree
Stick to one person as a lover, spouse or business partner, to wander causes only trouble

The community

As the individual is part of a family, he or she is also part of a community. The dependence of a person on his or her fellow human-beings and the strength that comes from uniting is expressed in various ways:

Kgosi ke kgosi ka setshaba
A king is a king through the nation
The power of a king or a leader comes from his subjects or followers

Motho ke motho ka motho yo mongwe
A person is a person through other people
A person becomes human through his or her interaction with other people;
"No man is an island"

Tshweu ga di tswane
Whites do not betray each other
White people never betray one another to outsiders

Molao o tsewa šudung or
Molao khutsana e o tsaya šudung
An orphan learns customs from the tribal ward
*Good advice and valuable teachings can be picked up
from the tribal ward (at informal community events)*

Fifing go tshwaranwa ka dikobo
In darkness, unity is through blankets
*People should stand together in times of distress; people
should close ranks in times of danger*

Bobedi bo bolaya noga
Two-some kill a snake
Together you overcome an enemy;
"Unity is strength"

Setshwarwa ke ntšwa pedi ga se thata
That which is attacked by two dogs
has no power
You cannot win against combined forces or a united front

The individual

People are interdependent. One should always be aware of how your situation in life may change. A number of proverbs warn against arrogance and remind us that no one knows what the future holds:

Lenao ga le na nko
The foot cannot smell (where it is going)
You do not know what may happen in the future, you may one day find yourself at the mercy of someone you treated badly when (s)he needed your help

O se tshege monkawena mareledi a sa le pele
Do not laugh at the fallen, the slippery (part) still lies ahead
Do not mock a friend in distress. As you do not know what the future holds for you, you may encounter similar problems later

Matsogo dinku a a thebana

Hands, like sheep, meet each other half-way

If you do someone a good turn today, that person will return the favour one day

Montsamaisa bosigo ke mo leboga bo sele

The one who accompanies me at night, I thank him in the day

A companion in distress will be thanked and appreciated when the crisis is over

Lefoko ga le boe go boa monoana

Only the finger returns, not the word

A spoken word cannot be taken back, only the finger you point with – so be careful not to utter words you may regret later

Human nature

As one can expect, a large number of proverbs reflect on human nature and the weaknesses human beings display:

Moipone ga a ipone selo mo tlhogong
The seer does not see something on his own head

One never recognises one's own shortcomings;
"Behold the log in your own eye before you notice the splinter in your brother's eye"

Mothudi ga a na thipa
The fixer has no knife

The tradesman does not have the tools or time to work for himself

As little children, we often made fun of a shoemaker whose shoes were always worn out. We would jeer, "Mothudi ga a na thipa!" and this gentleman would look at us in anger and frustration, and move on helplessly as we ran away

Phala e se nang phalana lesilo
An impala without its off-spring is a fool
A older person without a younger person around acts foolish

Moipolai ga a llelwe
People do not weep for one who kills himself
One with a deliberate self-inflicted injury deserves no sympathy from other people

Fa e swa e a raga
When it dies, it kicks
A helpless or doomed person acts violently;
"It is the last kicks of a dying horse"

Modiri o a lebala, modirwa ga a lebale
The doer forgets, the one done to never forgets
The one who hurts or harms soon forgets, the one hurt or harmed never forgets

IT IS INTERESTING that two seemingly good human charac-
teristics – being kind and being accepting – can, if overdone,
be the cause of self-destruction:

Pelo nomi e bolaile mmamasiloanoke
Generosity killed the hammerhead (bird)
*You can be destroyed by being overly kind-hearted, because
people often take advantage of others' kindness or generosity*

*Ngwana a sa lleng o swela tharing**
A child who does not cry, dies in the cradle
*If you suffer in silence, you may die unnoticed; suffering
in silence may lead to dying in silence. If you do not speak
your mind, you cannot change the situation for the better*

* *tharing is* the skin in which a baby is tied on to the mother's back

Beware of deception

As was pointed out earlier, there are many proverbs that caution and warn. As old as the hills, are the many reminders that "appearances are deceptive":

O se kgatlhwe ke none e feta
Do not admire a blesbuck passing by
*Fleeting impressions do not necessarily have lasting value –
so don't be attracted by a passing beauty*

O se bone thola borethe, teng ga yona go a baba

Do not adore the smoothness of the bitter-apple, it is acrid inside

Do not be deceived by a pleasing exterior, people can be deceitful

Nta ya se lomela kobong

A louse bites after hiding inside your blanket

Beware of a person who may misuse his or her position of closeness or friendship to harm you

Pelo kwa teng ke phuti
The heart inside is a duiker
*The face can conceal many things – you alone knows what
you harbour in your mind;
"Don't judge a book by its cover"*

Meno masweu polaa a tshega
White teeth kill with a giggle
A smile can hide a plot to harm you

Motlhala wa motho ke molomo
A person's route is his mouth
*You will only know the stranger at your door when (s)he
tells you who they are by introducing him or her to you*

SOMETIMES A PERSON may think that (s)he has deceived those around her or him, but, be careful:

Sekhukhuni se bonwa ke sebataladi
The prowler is seen by a person who hides by lying down flat
Be warned: mischievous deeds may be detected by an observer you do not notice

Moloi ga a mmala
A witch has no distinguishing colour
Be careful of those you deal with, you never know who they are

Don't despair

By the same token that some proverbs warn you of deceit, others offer consolation in times of hardship or suffering:

Mojamonna ga a mo fetse
That which eats a man does not finish him
No one can destroy a human being completely, because after someone's death her or his deeds and fame will remain

Se sa feleng se a tlhola
That which is boundless is fathomless
Nothing goes on forever; there is an end to everything, also suffering

Tsela kgopo ga e latse nageng
A round-about route does not let you sleep in

Tsela kgopo ga e latse nageng
A round-about route does not let you sleep in the veld
A winding road will also get a traveller to where (s)he wants to be

Lemme ga le bolaye, go bolaya lefifi
It is the darkness, not a small thing, that kills
The little you have is better than nothing, so look after the little you have

Tlhapi, solofela leraga bodiba bo tšhele o bo lebile
Fish, accept the mud, for the fountain has dried up before your eyes
Rely on and use the little that is still available to you because there is nothing else – this is often said to children whose parents have died

Botlhoko bo ntshiwa ka jo bongwe
Pain is relieved by pain
To get out of the hardship or poverty you find yourself in,
you have to toil and work very hard

Go bitsa go bitsa motho go bitse Modimo
Instead of calling man, call God
God can help where man fails

Don't blame others

Other proverbs contain advice for those individuals who prefer to blame others or refuse to accept responsibility:

Moromiwa ga a na lonya
The messenger carries no blame
Do not blame the messenger for bad news, he is not responsible for the situation, he only reports it

O se mpofelle polowana seropeng
Do not tie a small penis to my thigh
Do not implicate me unfairly or blame me for things I have not done;
"Do not pass the buck"

Ngaka e sa sweng e a eta

The traditional healer (doctor) who does not die journeys the world over to heal

Procrastination can cost you your life: for example, if you put off seeing the doctor, you may find him dead or gone on a visit when you finally need him

Motshega kgarebe ke moenyadi

Someone who makes fun of a maiden may be the one who marries her later

A young man often ends up marrying a maiden he has made fun of, in the same way one may find yourself doing what you were determined never to do

Mpepi e ya ipelegisa
Someone who does not care for other's
children will have to care for her own one day
To receive support, you need to give support

Se nkganang se nthola morwalo
The one who rejects me, relieves me of the
baggage
*If someone rejects you, it is not always so bad because they
rid you of any responsibility towards them*

"Look before you leap"
Other proverbs warn against hasty, impetuous behaviour:

Phuduhudu e thamo telele e batwa ke melamu e se ya yone
or *Phuduhudu e e molala moleele, e tshabelwa ke marumo*
A steenbok with a long neck is maimed by
spears not meant for it
*A forward person interferes in matters which do not concern
her or him*

Segatlhamelamasisi, le botsetsing se a tsena
A hero steps even into the accouchment section
(where women give birth)
*Said when someone interferes in sacred matters, or is too
forward;*
"Fools rush in where angels fear to tread"

WHEN THE ABOVE happens, one is tempted to say:

O batlile o bona marago a noga/tshwene!
You nearly saw the snake's/baboon's buttocks!
Said when someone narrowly escaped a tragic or nasty situation

Poela e ya ja
Vengeance devours
Returning to what you had earlier discarded as unworthy can ruin you, or perhaps: being set on revenge, you may destroy yourself

O tshwara nnyo gabedi ka letsogo
Do not grasp a vagina twice with your hand
Do not return to a situation which was nasty. Learn from your previous experience, for example, if a marriage has been bitter, think twice before remarrying

The rich and fortunate

The behaviour of those with wealth and status, and the confidence and independence that possessions give, have inspired a number of proverbs stating fact:

Moji ga a bope

The eater does not bellow

A man of wealth and stature does not indulge in idle boasting

Moja morago kgosi

The one who eats last is a king

Don't rejoice too soon;
"(S)he who laughs last laughs best"

EXPRESSING A SIMILAR sentiment but from a different angle, is the proverb:

Motlhopa ntshi ke yo o kgorang
Only the rich filter out the flies
Only a self-sufficient person can be choosey about what (s)he eats

Mphemphe e ya lapisa motho o kgonwa ke sa gagwe
Give, give is tiresome, a person is better off with his or her own possessions
Begging is a bother, it is better to be self-sufficient

Bojang jwa pitse ke jo bo mo mpeng
A horse owns only the grass in its stomach
*The most valuable things are those you have earned
and own*

Khudu ya mariga e itsiwe ke mmei
Winter's tortoise in known by its depositor
A precious treasure is known to its keeper

BUT BE WARNED, riches can be lost, because:

Khumo le lehuma di lala mmogo
Wealth and poverty go hand in hand
Those who possess wealth should never overlook or mock the poor, because they may easily lose their wealth and become poor themselves

Youth, age and death
A last group of proverbs concern the different phases through which a human being passes in his or her lifetime. About all the different stages there are lessons to be learnt:

Lore lo ojwa lo sa le metsi
A stick is bent while wet
A child is best trained when it is still young and tender;
"Bend the twig while it is still tender"

Thutela-bogolo e a roba
Educating an old person can break her or him
Acquiring new habits in old age can be harmful

Ngwana yo sa reetseng bagolo, o tla thanya lomapo lo le tsebeng

A child who does not heed the elders' warning will suffer the rapture of his or her eardrum

Children who are disobedient will meet tragedy or misfortune

Tlhale e fedile morutshing

The thread is running out, the reel is almost empty

Energy decreases with age

Loso lo mo mojeng wa kobo

Death is at the right-hand side of the blanket

Death is always close and can strike at any moment

Mano ga a site go sita a loso

Plans can always be made, except death's

You can devise means to get out of all sorts of trouble;
it is only death that you cannot avoid or outwit

Loso logolo ditshego

The main death is laughter

It is possible to find a moment for laughter in the
grimmest of situations

IN CONCLUSION, together, all the preceding proverbs teach one lesson:

Lesilo tsamaya le matlhale o tlhalefe
Fool, walk with the wise and be wise

The wise, in this case, are our own observant and wise ancestors who invented proverbs and used them to educate the young. Isn't it time for us, all South Africans, to start being proud of our heritage? Of the richness embedded in the proverbs that some of us still carry with us while others were never introduced to them?

Through proverbs we can address many of the difficult issues besetting our country; in the wisdom that has been handed down generation after generation, we can find solace and solutions. Through proverbs we can return to our culture, the culture of "Botho", of "Ubuntu" – the spirit of mutual respect and recognition.